MASTERING GERMAN SHEPHERD BREEDING

The Complete German Shepherd Breeder's Handbook: From choosing healthy parents to raising confident, well-adjusted puppies.

Ella M. Riggs

TABLE OF CONTENTS

INTRODUCTION

Welcome to "Mastering German Shepherd Breeding." I'm thrilled to share this practical guide with you, born out of my personal journey into the world of German shepherd breeding. No fancy words or complicated jargon here – just a straightforward account of how these incredible dogs inspired my pursuit.

It all started with a curious pup named Max. His boundless energy and unwavering loyalty sparked a passion within me to understand and contribute to the betterment of the German shepherd breed. This book is a culmination of the lessons learned, challenges faced, and successes achieved along the way.

As you embark on this journey with me, you'll find practical insights on selecting breeding stock, caring for pregnant dogs, nurturing healthy puppies, and navigating the ethical responsibilities of a breeder. But more than that, you'll discover the joy and fulfillment that comes from responsibly mastering the art of German shepherd breeding.

I invite you to dive into the pages ahead, where simplicity meets expertise. Whether you're a seasoned breeder or just starting, this book is a roadmap to success. Let's embark on this adventure together, fostering a community of passionate and responsible breeders. Your journey into mastering German shepherd breeding starts now – let's make it exceptional.

2

WHY YOU NEED A GERMAN SHEPHERD BREED IN YOUR HOME

This book on mastering German Shepherd breeding offers practical guidance for readers at various levels of experience. Whether you're a novice or an experienced breeder, you'll find valuable insights, including:

1. **Comprehensive Knowledge:** Gain a deep understanding of the German Shepherd breed, covering everything from their characteristics to genetic considerations.

2. **Practical Techniques:** Learn hands-on techniques for selecting quality breeding stock, caring for pregnant dogs, and ensuring the well-being of puppies from birth to early development.

3. **Ethical Breeding Practices:** Explore the ethical responsibilities of a breeder, promoting the health and welfare of the dogs throughout the breeding process.

4. **Nutritional Guidance:** Receive expert advice on nutrition for breeding dogs and puppies, ensuring their optimal health and development.

5. **Training and Socialization Strategies:** Discover effective strategies for training and socializing German Shepherds, contributing to their overall well-rounded development.

6. **Problem Prevention:** Understand common health issues and preventive care measures, helping you anticipate and address potential challenges.

7. **Responsible Breeding:** Emphasizing the importance of responsible breeding practices, the book encourages ethical considerations and responsible placement of puppies.

8. **Business Aspects:** Learn about marketing strategies and considerations for placing puppies, turning your passion into a fulfilling and responsible business.

9. **Continual Learning:** The book provides resources for ongoing education, ensuring that readers can stay informed and adapt to the evolving field of dog breeding.

10. **Inspiration and Motivation:** Through real-life case studies and success stories, the book aims to inspire and motivate readers on their journey to mastering German Shepherd breeding.

This comprehensive guide is not just about breeding dogs; it's a roadmap to becoming a responsible, knowledgeable, and successful breeder. Whether you're starting your breeding venture or refining existing skills, this book is designed to be a reliable companion throughout your journey.

A German Shepherd can be a valuable addition to your household for several reasons:

1. **Loyalty and Companionship:** German Shepherds are known for their unwavering loyalty and strong bond with their owners, making them excellent companions.
2. **Protective Instincts:** With a natural protective instinct, German Shepherds can serve as vigilant guardians for your home and family.
3. **Versatility:** Known for their versatility, German Shepherds excel in various roles, including family pets, working dogs, and service animals.
4. **Intelligence and Trainability**: German Shepherds are highly intelligent and trainable, making them adaptable to various tasks and activities.
5. **Exercise Partners:** Energetic and agile, German Shepherds thrive on physical activity. They make excellent exercise partners for outdoor activities, promoting a healthy lifestyle.
6. **Playful and Social:** Despite their protective nature, German Shepherds are often playful

and social, especially with proper socialization from an early age.

7. **Service and Assistance:** Many German Shepherds are trained as service dogs, assisting individuals with disabilities or special needs.

8. **Search and Rescue Abilities:** Their keen sense of smell and agility make German Shepherds valuable in search and rescue operations.

9. **Low Maintenance Grooming**: While they have a thick double coat, German Shepherds are relatively low-maintenance in terms of grooming compared to some other breeds.

10. **Family Integration:** German Shepherds often integrate well into family life, forming strong bonds with all members and providing a sense of security.

Before deciding to bring a German Shepherd into your home, it's essential to consider their needs, including proper training, exercise, and socialization. When these needs are met, a German Shepherd can become not just a pet but a cherished and integral part of your family.

3

UNDERSTANDING THE GERMAN SHEPHERD BREED

In delving into the world of the German Shepherd breed, it's crucial to appreciate the rich history and remarkable characteristics that define this beloved canine companion. My personal journey into understanding these intelligent and versatile dogs has been an enlightening experience, filled with unique insights that I'm excited to share.

Historical Roots:

The German Shepherd traces its lineage back to the late 19th century in Germany. Originally bred for herding, these dogs quickly showcased their exceptional intelligence and work ethic. German Shepherds gained prominence as police and military dogs due to their keen sense of loyalty and high trainability.

Appearance:

One cannot overlook the striking physical features of the German Shepherd. With a strong, well-muscled body, erect ears, and a distinctive double coat, they epitomize both elegance and strength. My own encounter with a German Shepherd left me captivated by its regal appearance, a testament to the breed's aesthetic allure.

Intelligence and Trainability:

One of the defining characteristics of German Shepherds is their unmatched intelligence. Their ability to quickly grasp commands and adapt to various tasks makes them a favorite in roles ranging from search and rescue to assistance work. My experience training a German Shepherd highlighted its eagerness to learn, responding positively to consistent and positive reinforcement.

Loyalty Beyond Measure:

German Shepherds are renowned for their unwavering loyalty to their human companions. My personal bond with one of these remarkable dogs reinforced this trait. Their loyalty extends beyond mere companionship; it becomes a profound connection that enriches the lives of both dog and owner.

Versatility in Roles:

The versatility of German Shepherds is truly remarkable. From excelling in obedience trials to showcasing their agility in canine sports, these dogs thrive in a variety of roles. My own exposure to their versatility came when witnessing a German Shepherd seamlessly transition from a playful family pet to a focused working dog, showcasing the breed's adaptability.

Exercise and Mental Stimulation:

German Shepherds are dynamic dogs that require both physical exercise and mental stimulation. Their boundless energy necessitates regular walks, playtime, and engaging activities to keep them content. My journey involved discovering creative ways to provide mental challenges, ensuring a happy and well-balanced German Shepherd.

Health Considerations:

While embracing the joys of having a German Shepherd companion, it's essential to be mindful of their health. Regular veterinary check-ups, a nutritious diet, and maintaining an active lifestyle contribute to their overall well-being. My own experiences underscored the importance of proactive healthcare in preserving the vitality of these magnificent dogs.

In conclusion, understanding the German Shepherd breed goes beyond superficial appreciation. It involves delving into their rich history, appreciating their physical and intellectual prowess, and nurturing the unique bond that forms between them and their human companions. My personal journey has been a testament to the profound connection one can cultivate with these extraordinary dogs, making the German Shepherd a breed that leaves an indelible mark on the hearts of those fortunate enough to share their lives with them.

4

SELECTING QUALITY BREEDING STOCK

Embarking on the journey of breeding German Shepherds demands a meticulous approach to selecting quality breeding stock. The choices made in this critical stage not only influence the immediate offspring but have a lasting impact on the breed's future. Drawing from my own experiences, I'll guide you through the essential considerations and decision-making process involved in choosing breeding stock.

Understanding the Breed Standard:

A foundational step in selecting breeding stock is a comprehensive understanding of the German Shepherd breed standard. This guideline outlines the desired physical and temperamental traits, serving as a blueprint for breeders. My own journey began with studying and internalizing this standard, ensuring a clear vision of the ideal German Shepherd.

Health Screening:

Healthy breeding stock is fundamental to producing robust and resilient litters. Prioritize health screenings for potential breeding dogs, including evaluations for hip and elbow dysplasia, genetic disorders, and overall physical wellness. My experience emphasized the significance of thorough health assessments, steering clear of potential hereditary issues and ensuring a strong foundation for future generations.

Temperament Evaluation:

The temperament of breeding stock is equally crucial. German Shepherds should exhibit traits like intelligence, trainability, and a balanced demeanor. Personal interactions with potential breeding dogs offered valuable insights into their temperamental qualities. Observing how they respond to various stimuli and their social behavior became a pivotal aspect of my selection process.

Pedigree Analysis:

A well-documented pedigree is akin to a family tree, providing insights into the lineage and genetic history of a dog. My own journey involved delving into pedigrees, tracing the ancestry of potential breeding stock. A strong pedigree enhances the likelihood of passing desirable traits to the offspring, contributing to the overall quality of the breeding program.

Conformation to Breed Standards:

Aligning breeding stock with the breed standard extends beyond health and temperament to include physical conformation. Assessing features such as body structure, coat quality, and gait ensures that the selected dogs embody the distinctive characteristics of the German Shepherd breed. My experiences taught me to appreciate the nuanced details that contribute to a well-structured and visually appealing dog.

Breeder's Ethics and Practices:

Collaborating with reputable breeders who adhere to ethical practices is paramount. My journey emphasized the importance of establishing a relationship with breeders who prioritize the well-being of the dogs, maintain transparency in their practices, and actively contribute to the betterment of the breed. This collaboration is essential in ensuring a responsible and sustainable breeding program.

Long-Term Vision:

Selecting quality breeding stock is not just about the present but entails a forward-thinking perspective. Consider the long-term implications of your choices on the breed's overall health, temperament, and conformation. My own experiences underscored the significance of planning for the future, with a commitment to maintaining and enhancing the integrity of the German Shepherd breed.

In conclusion, the selection of quality breeding stock is a pivotal aspect of responsible dog breeding. Drawing from my personal journey, I encourage breeders to approach this process with a holistic perspective, considering health, temperament, conformation, and ethical practices. By making informed choices in selecting breeding stock, we contribute to the preservation and improvement of the German Shepherd breed, ensuring a legacy of excellence for generations to come.

5

BREEDING ETHICS AND RESPONSIBILITIES

Embarking on the journey of breeding German Shepherds goes beyond the excitement of adorable puppies; it carries a profound responsibility to uphold ethical standards. Drawing from my own experiences, this chapter delves into the crucial aspects of breeding ethics and the responsibilities that come with nurturing new life.

Commitment to Health and Well-being:

Ethical breeding begins with a commitment to the health and well-being of both the breeding stock and their offspring. Regular veterinary check-ups, vaccinations, proper nutrition, and a clean living environment are non-negotiable components of responsible breeding. My own dedication to maintaining optimal health standards reinforced the importance of this foundational responsibility.

Selective Breeding Practices:

Selective breeding involves thoughtful and purposeful pairings to enhance desirable traits while mitigating potential health issues. My journey as a breeder emphasized the significance of resisting the temptation to prioritize superficial characteristics over the well-being of the dogs. Ethical breeding is rooted in a genuine concern for the overall welfare of the breed.

Puppy Placement with Care:

Responsible breeders prioritize the well-matched placement of puppies into suitable homes. Thorough screening of potential owners, clear communication about the breed's needs, and ongoing support are essential. My own experiences involved building lasting relationships with puppy buyers, ensuring a positive and supportive environment for the dogs throughout their lives.

Education and Transparency:

Ethical breeders prioritize education and transparency. Providing prospective owners with comprehensive information about the breed, the breeding process, and potential challenges fosters a sense of responsibility in new dog owners. My journey underscored the importance of being an accessible source of knowledge, guiding owners through the nuances of caring for a German Shepherd.

Responsible Marketing and Advertising:

Avoiding sensationalism and false promises in marketing is a key aspect of ethical breeding. My own commitment to honest representation in advertising emphasized the importance of setting realistic expectations for potential puppy buyers. Transparency builds trust and ensures a positive experience for both the new owners and the dogs.

Lifetime Responsibility for the Dogs:

Ethical breeders recognize their responsibility extends beyond the moment a puppy leaves for its new home. My experiences highlighted the importance of remaining a lifelong resource for puppy buyers, offering guidance and support as needed. This commitment ensures the well-being of the dogs throughout their entire lives.

Avoiding Overbreeding:

Overbreeding can lead to health issues and compromise the overall quality of the breed. Responsible breeders carefully plan and limit the number of litters to prevent overpopulation and safeguard the health of breeding stock. My own journey involved making intentional decisions about breeding frequency, prioritizing the welfare of the dogs over quantity.

Contributing to Breed Improvement:

Ethical breeders actively contribute to the improvement of the breed by staying informed about advancements in veterinary science, behavior training, and responsible breeding practices. My experiences reinforced the importance of continuous learning and adapting breeding strategies to contribute positively to the German Shepherd breed's overall betterment.

In conclusion, ethical breeding is a multifaceted commitment that involves a dedication to the health, well-being, and ethical treatment of the dogs. Drawing from personal experiences, this chapter emphasizes the responsibility that comes with bringing new life into the world and the enduring commitment required to ensure the happiness and welfare of the German Shepherd breed. Through ethical practices, breeders play a pivotal role in shaping a positive future for these remarkable dogs.

6

REPRODUCTIVE HEALTH AND CARE

Ensuring the reproductive health of your German Shepherd is essential for both breeders and pet owners. In this chapter, we'll explore practical tips for maintaining optimal reproductive health in these magnificent dogs without diving into complex jargon.

Regular Veterinary Check-ups:

Schedule routine veterinary check-ups to monitor your dog's overall health, including reproductive aspects. These visits help catch any potential issues early on and ensure that your German Shepherd is in prime condition for breeding or simply leading a healthy life.

Balanced Nutrition:

Providing a well-balanced diet is crucial for reproductive health. High-quality dog food with the right mix of nutrients supports overall well-being. Ensure that your dog maintains a healthy weight, as obesity can impact fertility. Consult your veterinarian to tailor the diet to your specific dog's needs.

Hygiene and Cleanliness:

Maintain good hygiene, especially during the breeding process. Keep the living area clean to prevent infections. Regularly check for any signs of discomfort, discharge, or unusual behavior that might indicate reproductive issues.

Understanding the Estrous Cycle:

For breeders, understanding the estrous cycle is key. Female dogs typically go into heat twice a year, and recognizing the signs is essential for successful breeding. Keep a calendar to track cycles and plan mating accordingly.

Monitoring Heat Cycles:

During the heat cycle, monitor your female dog closely for behavioral changes, swelling of the vulva, and a bloody discharge. Male dogs may show increased interest during this time. If you're planning to breed, it's crucial to know the optimal time for mating, usually around the 11th to 13th day of the heat cycle.

Consulting a Reproductive Specialist:

If you encounter challenges or are planning a significant breeding program, consider consulting a reproductive specialist. These veterinarians have expertise in fertility, breeding techniques, and can provide valuable guidance to enhance the chances of a successful mating.

Preventing Unwanted Pregnancies:

For pet owners who don't intend to breed, spaying or neutering your German Shepherd is a responsible choice. This not only prevents unwanted pregnancies but also offers health benefits, reducing the risk of certain reproductive-related diseases.

Addressing Infertility Concerns:

If you're experiencing difficulties in achieving pregnancy, consult your veterinarian. Infertility issues can stem from various factors, such as hormonal imbalances or structural abnormalities. A professional assessment can help identify the root cause and guide you towards appropriate solutions.

Post-Breeding Care:

After a successful mating, provide extra care to the pregnant female. Ensure she receives proper nutrition, moderate exercise, and a comfortable whelping area as she approaches delivery. Familiarize yourself with the signs of labor to be ready for the birthing process.

Monitoring Pregnancy Progress:

Regular veterinary check-ups are crucial during pregnancy to monitor the health of both the mother and the developing puppies. Ultrasound examinations and X-rays can provide valuable insights into the litter's size and health.

In conclusion, maintaining reproductive health in German Shepherds involves a combination of regular veterinary care, proper nutrition, and attentive monitoring. Whether you're a breeder or a pet owner, these practical tips contribute to the overall well-being of your dog and, if applicable, the success of any breeding endeavors. Always remember that a healthy dog is a happy dog, and a well-cared-for German Shepherd can bring joy and fulfillment to your life.

PREGNANCY AND WHELPING

Welcoming a new generation of German Shepherd puppies into the world is an exciting and rewarding experience. In this chapter, we'll explore practical tips for navigating through pregnancy and the whelping process in a straightforward manner, avoiding complex jargon.

Prenatal Care:

Once you've confirmed your German Shepherd is pregnant, continue regular veterinary check-ups.

These visits help monitor the health of the expecting mother and her developing puppies. Discuss nutritional needs and any specific care requirements with your vet.

Nutrition During Pregnancy:

Adjust the pregnant dog's diet to meet increased nutritional demands. High-quality puppy or all-life-stages food, as recommended by your vet, supports the mother's health and the proper development of the growing puppies. Regular feeding schedules are crucial for stability.

Provide a Comfortable Whelping Area:

Prepare a quiet, comfortable, and warm area for whelping. A box with sides high enough to prevent drafts but low enough for the mother to easily access is ideal. Line it with soft, clean bedding, and ensure it's placed in a quiet, private space.

Monitoring Body Temperature:

As the due date approaches, monitor the pregnant dog's body temperature. A sudden drop may indicate labor is imminent. Regular checks will help you predict when the whelping process is likely to begin.

Recognizing Signs of Labor:

Understanding the signs of labor is crucial. Restlessness, nesting behavior, and a decrease in body temperature are common indicators. The mother may also become more vocal and display signs of discomfort. If you observe these behaviors, it's time to prepare for the arrival of the puppies.

Assisting During Whelping:

Most dogs handle the birthing process naturally, but be ready to assist if needed. Provide gentle encouragement and comfort to the mother. If a pup is stuck in the birth canal for an extended period or if complications arise, contact your veterinarian immediately.

Caring for Newborn Puppies:

Once the puppies are born, ensure they are breathing and nursing well. Keep the whelping area warm and free from drafts. Monitor the mother to ensure she is attentive to the needs of her offspring. If assistance is required, consult your vet promptly.

First Veterinary Check-up for Puppies:

Schedule a veterinary check-up for the newborn puppies within a few days of birth. This guarantees early detection of any possible health problems.

Discuss vaccination schedules, deworming, and general care guidelines with your vet.

Weaning Process:

Around three to four weeks, you can introduce solid food to the puppies alongside nursing. Gradually transition them to puppy food. Monitor their progress closely, adjusting their diet as needed.

Post-Whelping Care for the Mother:

After whelping, the mother requires attentive care. Provide her with a nutritious diet, fresh water, and a quiet space for rest. Keep a close eye for any signs of postpartum complications and seek veterinary assistance if needed.

Socialization and Early Training:

As the puppies grow, start gentle socialization and basic training. Introduce them to different situations, people, and things. This foundation sets the stage for well-adjusted adult dogs.

In conclusion, navigating through pregnancy and the whelping process requires a blend of attentive care, preparation, and a keen eye for signs of distress. Whether you're a seasoned breeder or a first-time pet owner, these practical tips aim to guide you through this remarkable journey, ensuring the health and well-being of both the mother and her adorable German Shepherd puppies.

8

EARLY PUPPY CARE DEVELOPMENT

Bringing a new German Shepherd puppy into your home marks the beginning of a rewarding journey. This chapter outlines practical tips for early puppy care and development, focusing on straightforward advice without delving into complex jargon.

Nutrition:

Start your puppy off right with a high-quality puppy food recommended by your veterinarian. Puppies grow rapidly, and proper nutrition is essential for their development. Follow feeding guidelines, and monitor their weight to ensure they are on a healthy trajectory.

Scheduled Feeding:

Establish a consistent feeding schedule. Puppies thrive on routine, and regular meals help with housebreaking and maintaining a stable digestive system. Remove uneaten food after about 20 minutes to create a routine for your pup.

Potty Training:

When it comes to potty training, consistency is essential. Get your puppy outside as much as possible, particularly after meals and upon waking. Praise them when they go outside, reinforcing the idea that this is the desired behavior. Be patient, accidents happen, and positive reinforcement goes a long way.

Socialization:

Expose your puppy to various people, places, and experiences. Early socialization helps them become well-adjusted adults. Introduce them to different environments, sounds, and friendly people to build their confidence.

Basic Training Commands:

Commence with simple directives such as sit, stay, and come. Use positive reinforcement, such as treats or praise, to encourage good behavior. Short training sessions with positive interactions create a foundation for lifelong learning.

Veterinary Care:

Make time for routine veterinary examinations to keep an eye on your puppy's health. Keep up with vaccinations, deworming, and any preventive care recommended by your vet. It's critical to identify possible health problems early.

Grooming Routine:

Introduce your puppy to grooming early on. Brush their coat regularly, check ears, trim nails, and get them used to baths. This creates a positive association with grooming and makes it easier as they grow.

Safe and Stimulating Environment:

Create a safe space for your puppy to explore. Remove hazards, secure electrical cords, and provide appropriate toys. Mental stimulation is as important as physical activity for a growing pup.

Crate Training:

Introduce your puppy to a crate as a safe and comfortable space. Crate training aids in housebreaking and provides security. Make it a positive experience, associating the crate with treats, toys, and a cozy bed.

Teething and Chewing:

Puppies explore the world with their mouths, and teething can be uncomfortable. To relieve their gums, give them the right chew toys. Rotate toys to keep them engaged and discourage inappropriate chewing.

Building Trust and Bonding:

Spend quality time bonding with your puppy. Gentle play, cuddling, and positive interactions build trust. A strong bond contributes to a well-adjusted and happy adult dog.

Regular Exercise:

German Shepherd puppies are energetic and require regular exercise. Play fetch, go for walks, and provide opportunities for mental stimulation. Be mindful not to overexert young joints, adjusting the intensity as they grow.

In conclusion, early puppy care lays the foundation for a healthy, well-behaved, and happy adult dog. Whether you're a first-time pet owner or a seasoned dog enthusiast, these practical tips aim to guide you through the early stages of your German Shepherd puppy's life, ensuring a positive and fulfilling journey for both of you.

9

NUTRITION FOR BREEDING DOGS AND PUPPIES

Ensuring the right nutrition for breeding dogs and their puppies is vital for their health and development. In this chapter, we'll discuss practical tips in clear language without delving into complex jargon.

Breeding Dogs:

High-Quality Dog Food:

1. Feed your breeding dogs a high-quality, well-balanced dog food. Look for options designed for reproduction or all life stages, as they provide the necessary nutrients for breeding dogs.

Protein and Fat Levels:

2. Opt for dog food with adequate protein and fat levels. Protein supports the development

of healthy tissues, while fat provides essential energy. Check with your veterinarian to ensure the food meets the specific needs of breeding dogs.

Supplements:

3. Discuss the need for supplements with your vet. While a balanced diet is crucial, breeding dogs might benefit from additional supplements like folic acid or omega-3 fatty acids. Avoid self-prescribing and seek professional advice.

Maintain an Ideal Body Condition:

4. Monitor your breeding dog's weight closely. Maintaining an ideal body condition is essential for reproductive health. Consult your veterinarian to establish a feeding plan that keeps your dog in optimal shape.

Pregnant and Nursing Dogs:

Increased Caloric Intake:

1. Adjust the diet of pregnant and nursing dogs to accommodate increased caloric needs. During these periods, they require more energy to support their own health and the growth of developing puppies.

High-Quality Puppy Food:

2. Transition pregnant and nursing dogs to a high-quality puppy food during the later stages of pregnancy and throughout lactation. Puppy food provides the extra nutrients needed for the developing puppies.

Small, Frequent Meals:

3. Offer smaller, more frequent meals to prevent discomfort or bloating. This can be especially important for pregnant dogs as the growing puppies occupy more space in the abdomen.

Hydration:

4. Ensure access to fresh water at all times. Adequate hydration is crucial for pregnant and nursing dogs. Dehydration can impact milk production and overall health.

Puppy Nutrition:

Puppy-Specific Food:

1. Transition puppies to a high-quality puppy-specific food around 4–6 weeks of age. Puppy food is formulated to meet the unique nutritional needs of growing dogs.

Balanced Diet:

2. Provide a balanced diet to support proper growth and development. Puppy food should contain essential nutrients like calcium and phosphorus for bone development.

Gradual Transition to Adult Food:

3. Gradually transition puppies to adult food based on your veterinarian's recommendation. A gradual changeover helps prevent upset stomach.

Avoid Overfeeding:

4. While it's tempting to indulge those adorable puppy eyes, avoid overfeeding. Follow feeding guidelines, monitor their weight, and adjust portions as needed to maintain a healthy body condition.

In conclusion, nutrition plays a crucial role in the health and well-being of breeding dogs and their puppies. By choosing high-quality food, adjusting diets based on life stages, and seeking professional guidance, you can ensure that your German Shepherds receive the nutrition they need for a happy and healthy life.

10

SOCIALIZATION AND TRAINING STRATEGIES

Socialization and training are essential aspects of raising a well-behaved and balanced German Shepherd. In this chapter, we'll explore practical tips for both in a straightforward manner, avoiding complex jargon.

Socialization:

Early Exposure:

1. Begin socialization early. Introduce your German Shepherd puppy to various environments, people, and other animals. Exposing them to different stimuli during their critical developmental periods helps build confidence.

Positive Experiences:

2. Create positive associations. Reward your puppy with treats, praise, or play when they encounter new situations. This reinforces positive behavior and helps them view new experiences as enjoyable.

Gradual Exposure:

3. Take it slow. Gradually expose your puppy to different environments and situations. Rushing the process can overwhelm them.

Focus on creating positive, stress-free interactions.

People and Other Pets:

4. Encourage positive interactions with people and other pets. Arrange playdates, visits to friends' houses, and encounters with friendly dogs. This helps your German Shepherd become comfortable with a diverse range of individuals.

Training Strategies:

Consistency is Key:

1. Be consistent with commands and expectations. Use the same cues for desired behaviors, and ensure everyone in your household follows the same rules. Consistency helps your German Shepherd understand what is expected.

Positive Reinforcement:

2. Emphasize positive reinforcement. Give out toys, praise, or treats for good behavior. This approach motivates your dog to repeat positive actions and builds a strong bond between you and your German Shepherd.

Clear Communication:

3. Use clear and simple commands. German Shepherds respond well to clear communication. Keep commands straightforward and consistent, avoiding confusing language. Use a firm but gentle tone.

Basic Commands:

4. Pay attention to basic instructions such as sit, remain, come, and leave it. Mastering these basics establishes a foundation for more advanced training and ensures a well-behaved companion.

Patience and Persistence:

5. Training takes time. Be patient and persistent. Dogs learn at their own rate much like people do. If your German Shepherd doesn't grasp a command immediately, stay patient and continue practicing.

Regular Sessions:

6. Conduct short, regular training sessions. Consistency is more effective than lengthy, sporadic training. Short sessions, especially during puppyhood, maintain your dog's interest and prevent them from getting bored.

Interactive Play:

7. Incorporate training into playtime. Interactive games like fetch or hide-and-seek can reinforce commands while providing mental stimulation and physical exercise.

Training Tools:

8. Utilize training tools if needed. Treats, clickers, and training collars can aid in reinforcing positive behavior. However, use these tools responsibly and ensure they align with positive training principles.

Professional Training Classes:

9. Consider professional training classes. Enrolling in obedience classes with a qualified trainer provides structured guidance and socialization opportunities for your German Shepherd.

Adapt to Your Dog's Personality:

10. Tailor your approach to your dog's personality. Some German Shepherds may respond better to certain training methods or motivation techniques. Adapt your strategy based on what resonates with your individual dog.

In conclusion, socialization and training are ongoing processes that contribute to a well-adjusted and obedient German Shepherd. By introducing positive experiences early, being consistent in training, and adapting your approach to your dog's personality, you set the stage for a harmonious relationship with your intelligent and loyal companion.

11

GENETIC CONSIDERATIONS IN BREEDING

Understanding genetic factors is crucial for responsible dog breeding. In this chapter, we'll delve into practical tips for genetic considerations in a straightforward manner, avoiding complex jargon.

Research Pedigrees:

Dive into Pedigree Analysis:

1. Before breeding, thoroughly research the pedigrees of potential breeding dogs. Understand the lineage, health history, and any prevalent genetic conditions within the bloodline. This information guides informed breeding decisions.

Screen for Inherited Diseases:

2. Prioritize health screenings for common genetic disorders in the breed. Testing for

conditions like hip and elbow dysplasia, progressive retinal atrophy, and certain cardiac issues helps in minimizing the risk of passing on genetic diseases.

Diversify Genetic Pool:
3. Avoid Close Inbreeding:

While line-breeding can strengthen desirable traits, avoid close inbreeding to minimize the risk of genetic disorders. Introducing genetic diversity by selecting mates from different bloodlines can contribute to a healthier and more resilient population.

Understand Carrier Status:

4. Be aware of carrier status for recessive genetic conditions. While carriers may not show symptoms, breeding two carriers can produce affected offspring. Genetic testing helps identify carriers and guides responsible breeding choices.

Selective Breeding Practices:
5. Prioritize Health Over Appearance:

In breeding, prioritize health and temperament over physical appearance. Aesthetic traits are important, but a focus on overall well-being contributes to a stronger and more sustainable breed.

Breeding Age Considerations:

6. Be mindful of breeding age. While German Shepherds may physically mature by one year, it's advisable to wait until they are at least two years old before breeding. This allows for proper skeletal and reproductive development.

Breeding Ethics:
7. Responsible Breeding Frequency:

Avoid overbreeding. Allow ample time between litters to ensure the health and well-being of the breeding dogs. Frequent breeding can strain the mother and increase the risk of genetic and reproductive issues.

Open Communication with Owners:

8. Maintain open communication with puppy
    buyers. Provide information about genetic
    testing, health clearances, and any known
    genetic conditions within the breeding lines.
    This transparency fosters trust and
    responsible ownership.

Consult with Veterinary Professionals:
9. Collaborate with Veterinarians:

Engage with veterinary professionals who specialize
in genetics. Regular consultations with a

veterinarian can help interpret genetic testing results, guide breeding decisions, and contribute to the overall health of the breeding program.

Continuous Learning:
10. Stay Informed About Breed Genetics:

Stay abreast of developments in breed genetics. Attend seminars, workshops, and conferences to enhance your understanding of genetic considerations in breeding. Continuous learning contributes to responsible breeding practices.

In conclusion, genetic considerations are paramount in maintaining a healthy and resilient German Shepherd breed. Thorough pedigree analysis, health screenings, selective breeding practices, and collaboration with veterinary professionals contribute to responsible breeding. By prioritizing genetic health, breeders play a crucial role in safeguarding the future well-being of these beloved dogs.

12

COMMON HEALTH ISSUES AND PREVENTIVE CARE

Maintaining the health of your German Shepherd is vital for a happy and fulfilling life. In this chapter, we'll discuss practical tips for recognizing and preventing common health issues in straightforward language, avoiding complex jargon.

Hip Dysplasia:

Observation and Early Intervention:

1. Keep an eye on your German Shepherd's gait and behavior. If you notice signs of discomfort or reluctance to move, consult your veterinarian promptly. Early intervention, including weight management and joint supplements, can help manage hip dysplasia.

Maintain Healthy Weight:

2. Weight management is crucial. Maintaining a healthy weight reduces stress on the joints and can contribute to preventing or managing hip dysplasia. For advice on a suitable diet and activity regimen, speak with your veterinarian.

Gastrointestinal Issues:
3. Balanced Diet:

Make sure your dog eats a healthy, well-balanced diet. High-quality dog food, appropriate portion sizes, and regular feeding schedules contribute to a healthy digestive system. Avoid feeding them human food that may upset their stomach.

Hydration:

4. Provide access to fresh water at all times. Proper hydration supports digestion and helps prevent issues like constipation. Dehydration can lead to various health problems, so always ensure your dog drinks enough water.

Skin Conditions:
5. Regular Grooming:

Regular grooming is essential. Brush your German Shepherd's coat to remove loose hair and prevent matting. Check for any signs of skin irritation, lumps, or parasites during grooming sessions.

Bathing:

6. Bathe your dog as needed but avoid excessive bathing, which can strip the skin of natural oils. Use a dog-friendly shampoo, and thoroughly dry their coat to prevent moisture-related skin issues.

Ear Infections:
7. Ear Cleaning:

Keep your dog's ears clean. Look for indications of swelling, redness, or bad smell. Use a veterinarian-recommended ear cleaner and gently clean the ears to prevent infections. Don't put things too far into the ear canal.

Regular Veterinary Check-ups:

8. Schedule regular veterinary check-ups. Professional examinations help identify potential health issues, including ear infections, before they escalate. Early detection allows for prompt treatment.

Preventive Veterinary Care:
9. Vaccinations and Deworming:

Stay current on vaccinations and deworming. Following a vet-recommended schedule helps protect your German Shepherd from common diseases and parasites.

Regular Dental Care:

10. Prioritize dental health. Use toothpaste and a toothbrush designed specifically for dogs to frequently brush your dog's teeth. Dental treats and toys designed to promote oral health can also be beneficial.

Exercise-Related Issues:
11. Appropriate Exercise:

Provide regular but appropriate exercise. German Shepherds are active dogs, but excessive exercise, especially during growth phases, can lead to joint issues. Tailor exercise to your dog's age, fitness level, and overall health.

Avoid Overexertion:

12. Be cautious of overexertion, especially in hot weather. German Shepherds are prone to overheating, which can lead to heatstroke.

Provide shade, water, and avoid vigorous exercise during the hottest parts of the day.

In conclusion, being proactive about your German Shepherd's health is key to preventing common issues. Regular observation, a balanced diet, proper grooming, preventive veterinary care, and appropriate exercise contribute to a healthy and happy life for your canine companion. Always consult your veterinarian for personalized advice based on your dog's specific needs and conditions.

13

RESPONSIBLE BREEDING PRACTICES

Responsible breeding is a commitment to the well-being of the dogs and the preservation of the breed's integrity. In this chapter, we'll explore practical tips for responsible breeding in clear and straightforward language.

Thorough Research:

Understanding Breed Standards:

1. Before starting a breeding program, thoroughly understand the breed standards for German Shepherds. This knowledge guides your breeding choices, ensuring that each litter contributes positively to the breed's characteristics.

Pedigree Analysis:

2. Research the pedigrees of potential breeding dogs. Examine health histories, genetic backgrounds, and any prevalent conditions within the bloodline. This information informs responsible breeding decisions.

Health Testing:
3. Comprehensive Health Screening:

Prioritize comprehensive health screenings for breeding dogs. Test for common genetic conditions, hip and elbow dysplasia, and other breed-specific health concerns. This proactive approach minimizes the risk of passing on hereditary diseases.

Regular Veterinary Check-ups:

4. Schedule regular veterinary check-ups for breeding dogs. These check-ups go beyond reproductive health, addressing overall well-being. Early detection of health issues ensures the breeding dogs are in optimal condition.

Selective Pairing:
5. Consider Genetic Diversity:

Avoid close inbreeding to maintain genetic diversity. Pairing dogs from different bloodlines reduces the risk of inherited disorders. Responsible breeders prioritize the health and longevity of the breed over cosmetic traits.

Balance Appearance and Function:

6. While adhering to breed standards, prioritize health and functionality over appearance. Aesthetic traits are essential, but responsible breeding focuses on producing dogs that are not only visually appealing but also physically and mentally sound.

Puppy Placement:
7. Thorough Screening of Homes:

Screen potential puppy buyers thoroughly. Ensure they understand the responsibilities of dog ownership and the specific needs of a German Shepherd. A responsible breeder places puppies in homes suited to their energy levels, training requirements, and overall well-being.

Lifetime Support:

8. Provide ongoing support to puppy buyers. A responsible breeder remains a resource throughout the dog's life, offering guidance, advice, and assistance whenever needed. This commitment ensures the well-being of the dogs even after they leave the breeder's care.

Ethical Marketing:
9. Transparent Communication:

Practice transparent communication in advertising. Avoid exaggerations or misleading statements about your dogs. Responsible breeders provide accurate information, set realistic expectations, and build trust with potential puppy buyers.

Educational Outreach:

10. Engage in educational outreach. Responsible breeders actively contribute to the betterment of the breed by sharing knowledge, participating in events, and educating the public about responsible dog ownership and breeding practices.

Limited Breeding Frequency:
11. Avoid Overbreeding:

Avoid overbreeding to prevent health issues and maintain the quality of the breed. Responsible breeders carefully plan and limit the number of litters each breeding dog produces, prioritizing the well-being of the dogs over quantity.

Retirement Planning:

12. Plan for the retirement of breeding dogs.
    Responsible breeders ensure that their
    breeding dogs enjoy a comfortable retirement,
    whether in their own homes or carefully
    selected forever homes.

In conclusion, responsible breeding is a multifaceted
commitment that involves thorough research, health
testing, selective pairing, responsible puppy
placement, ethical marketing, and a focus on the
well-being of both the dogs and their future owners.
By adopting these practices, breeders play a pivotal
role in maintaining the health, temperament, and
integrity of the German Shepherd breed.

14

RECORD-KEEPING AND DOCUMENTATION

Maintaining accurate records is a cornerstone of responsible dog breeding. In this chapter, we'll explore practical tips for record-keeping and documentation in straightforward language, avoiding complex jargon.

Individual Dog Records:

Create Individual Files:

1. For each dog in your breeding program, maintain a separate file. Include essential details such as pedigree information, health records, veterinary check-ups, and a timeline of vaccinations. This file serves as a comprehensive reference for each dog's history.

Microchip and Identification Details:

2. Note microchip information and any other
    forms of identification. This ensures a reliable
    method of identifying individual dogs,
    especially when it comes to health records
    and lineage verification.

Breeding Pairs and Litters:
3. Pairing Documentation:

Document each breeding pair, noting the date of
mating, method of breeding, and any relevant
details. This information helps track successful
pairings and identifies patterns for future breeding
decisions.

Litter Records:

4. Maintain detailed records for each litter,
    including birthdates, individual puppy
    identification, weight tracking, and any
    observed health issues. This information aids
    in providing accurate details to potential
    puppy buyers and informs future breeding
    choices.

Health Records:
5. Regular Veterinary Check-ups:

Record dates and details of regular veterinary check-ups. Include vaccinations, health screenings, and any recommended treatments. This establishes a comprehensive health history for each dog in your breeding program.

Medication and Treatment Logs:

6. Keep logs of any medications or treatments administered. Include dosage, frequency, and the reason for treatment. This documentation is essential for tracking the health of

individual dogs and ensuring appropriate care.

Reproductive Records:
7. Heat Cycles and Mating Dates:

Document the heat cycles of female dogs and the corresponding mating dates. This information is crucial for predicting due dates and planning future breedings.

Ultrasounds and Whelping Details:

8. If applicable, record ultrasound results during pregnancy and details of the whelping process. This helps track the reproductive health of your breeding dogs and aids in identifying any patterns or concerns.

Pedigree and Lineage Records:
9. Pedigree Information:

Maintain accurate pedigree information for each dog in your breeding program. This includes names, registration numbers, and any titled achievements. Pedigree records are vital for understanding the lineage and genetic background of your dogs.

Genetic Testing Results:

10. Keep records of genetic testing results for
    each dog. Note whether they are clear,
    carriers, or affected by specific conditions.
    This information guides responsible breeding
    decisions to minimize the risk of passing on
    hereditary diseases.

Communication Records:
11. Puppy Buyer Correspondence:

Save records of communication with puppy buyers.
Include details about puppy placements, health
guarantees, and any agreements. This ensures clarity
and transparency in your dealings with new dog
owners.

Educational Outreach:

12. Document your efforts in educational
    outreach, such as seminars, workshops, or
    articles. This showcases your commitment to
    continuous learning and sharing knowledge
    within the breeding community.

In conclusion, thorough record-keeping and documentation are vital for responsible dog breeding. Whether it's individual dog records, breeding pair information, health records, or communication logs, maintaining organized and accurate documentation contributes to the overall success and integrity of a breeding program. Adopting these practices ensures that breeders can make informed decisions and provide the best possible care for their dogs.

15

MARKETING AND PLACING PUPPIES

Successfully finding loving homes for your German Shepherd puppies involves effective marketing and careful placement. In this chapter, we'll explore practical tips for these crucial aspects of responsible breeding, using clear and straightforward language.

Building an Online Presence:

Create a Dedicated Website or Page:

1. Establish an online presence for your breeding program. A simple website or social media page provides a platform to showcase your dogs, share information about your breeding philosophy, and connect with potential puppy buyers.

Quality Photographs and Descriptions:

2. Present your puppies in the best light. Use high-quality photographs that capture their personalities. Accompany the images with clear and concise descriptions highlighting their traits, temperament, and any notable features.

Engaging with Potential Buyers:
3. Respond Promptly to Inquiries:

Timely communication is crucial. Respond promptly to enquiries from potential buyers. Provide detailed information about the puppies, parents, health clearances, and any relevant details. Clear communication builds trust.

Video Calls and Virtual Meetings:

4. Embrace technology for virtual interactions. Schedule video calls or virtual meetings with potential buyers. This allows them to see the puppies, ask questions, and get a feel for your breeding environment.

Educational Marketing:
5. Educational Content:

Share educational content about the breed. Write articles, create videos, or host webinars that offer insights into German Shepherd care, training, and breed-specific characteristics. This positions you as an expert and attracts like-minded, informed buyers.

Regular Updates:

6. Keep potential buyers informed with regular updates. Share milestones, such as puppy growth, training achievements, and health check-ups. Regular communication maintains interest and engagement.

Networking with Local Communities:
7. Engage with Local Events:

Attend local dog shows, events, or community gatherings. Networking within local communities introduces your breeding program to potential buyers who prefer local breeders. It also helps build a positive reputation within the community.

Collaborate with Veterinarians and Pet Stores:

8. Establish relationships with local veterinarians and pet stores. Display informational brochures or business cards at these locations. Veterinarians often interact with prospective dog owners, making it a valuable referral source.

Screening and Placing Puppies:
9. Application Process:

Implement a thorough application process. Require potential buyers to complete a detailed application form. This helps you understand their lifestyle, experience with dogs, and expectations, ensuring a good match between the puppy and its new family.

Home Visits or Video Tours:

10. Consider home visits or virtual video tours. This provides insights into the environment where the puppy will be raised. Ensure it's a safe and suitable place for a German Shepherd.

Post-Placement Support:
11. Provide Detailed Care Instructions:

Offer comprehensive care instructions to new puppy owners. Include information on feeding, grooming, training tips, and recommended veterinary care. This empowers new owners to care for their puppies effectively.

Lifetime Support:

12. Assure new owners of your ongoing support. Encourage them to reach out with questions or concerns at any time. This commitment fosters a positive relationship and emphasizes your dedication to the well-being of the puppies.

In conclusion, marketing and placing puppies require a combination of effective online presence, engaging with potential buyers, educational outreach, networking, and careful screening processes. By adopting these practices, responsible breeders enhance their chances of finding loving homes that align with the well-being of the German Shepherd puppies.

16

CONTINUING EDUCATION FOR BREEDERS

Staying informed and continuously expanding your knowledge is crucial for any responsible dog breeder. In this chapter, we'll explore practical tips for ongoing education in clear and straightforward language.

Attend Breed-Specific Events:

Dog Shows and Conformation Events:

1. Attend dog shows and conformation events specific to the German Shepherd breed. Observing expert judges and interacting with experienced breeders provides valuable insights into breed standards, traits, and evolving practices.

Breed Club Meetings:

2. Join local or national breed clubs and attend their meetings. These gatherings facilitate networking with other breeders, exchange of knowledge, and exposure to guest speakers who share their expertise on various aspects of responsible breeding.

Utilize Online Resources:
3. Webinars and Online Courses:

Participate in webinars and online courses. Many reputable organizations and breed clubs offer educational resources online. Topics can range from health and genetics to whelping and puppy rearing.

Discussion Forums and Social Media Groups:

4. Engage in online discussions. Join breed-specific forums and social media groups where breeders share experiences, ask questions, and discuss new developments. This informal exchange can be a rich source of practical knowledge.

Read Widely:
5. Books and Publications:

Read books and publications on dog breeding. Covering topics from breeding ethics to health management, well-researched literature can deepen your understanding and provide valuable perspectives.

Subscribe to Journals and Magazines:

6. Subscribe to dog-related journals and magazines. Stay updated on the latest research, advancements, and trends in the dog breeding community. Regular reading

keeps you informed about evolving best practices.

Network with Veterinary Professionals:
7. Attend Veterinary Seminars:

Attend seminars hosted by veterinary professionals. These events cover a range of topics, from reproductive health to genetic advancements. Building a rapport with veterinarians enhances your ability to interpret and apply medical knowledge in your breeding program.

Collaborate with Specialists:

8. Collaborate with veterinary specialists. Establish relationships with professionals specializing in areas such as genetics, reproductive health, or orthopedics. Their expertise can provide targeted insights relevant to your breeding goals.

Participate in Practical Workshops:
9. Breeding Workshops and Hands-On Training:

Enroll in breeding workshops and hands-on training sessions. Practical experience, guided by experts, enhances your skills in areas like whelping assistance, grooming, and puppy socialization.

Canine Behavior Courses:

10. Understand canine behavior. Courses focusing on dog behavior provide valuable knowledge for breeding dogs with stable temperaments. This understanding contributes to the well-being of your dogs and the success of your breeding program.

Seek Mentorship:
11. Mentorship Programs:

Join mentorship programs or seek guidance from experienced breeders. Learning from those with extensive experience provides practical insights, personalized advice, and a support system for navigating challenges.

Networking with Senior Breeders:

12. Network with senior breeders. Attend events where seasoned breeders gather, and take the opportunity to learn from their experiences. Building relationships with established breeders can open doors to continuous learning.

In conclusion, continuing education is a dynamic and ongoing process for responsible breeders. By actively participating in breed-specific events, utilizing online resources, reading, networking with veterinary professionals, participating in practical workshops, and seeking mentorship, you can stay at the forefront of responsible breeding practices. This commitment to learning contributes to the well-being of your dogs and the overall improvement of the German Shepherd breed.

17

CASE STUDIES AND SUCCESS STORIES

Examining case studies and success stories from experienced breeders can offer valuable insights and practical lessons for those in the world of German Shepherd breeding. In this chapter, we'll explore the benefits of studying real-life examples in clear and straightforward language.

Learning from Real Experiences:

Identifying Challenges:

1. Case studies shed light on challenges breeders have faced. By understanding these challenges, you can proactively implement strategies to address or avoid similar issues in your breeding program.

Problem-Solving Approaches:

2. Successful case studies often outline problem-solving approaches. These practical strategies can inspire effective solutions to common breeding dilemmas, contributing to the overall success of your program.

Breeding Practices:
3. Best Practices in Genetics:

Case studies can highlight successful genetic practices. Whether it's avoiding common hereditary issues or introducing innovative genetic testing, these stories offer tangible examples of responsible breeding practices.

Health Management Protocols:

4. Examining health-related case studies provides insights into effective health management protocols. Learn about preventive measures, early detection of health issues, and successful treatment plans.

Understanding Pedigree Dynamics:
5. Pedigree Influence on Traits:

Case studies often showcase the influence of pedigrees on desirable traits. By analyzing these examples, you can gain a deeper understanding of how specific bloodlines contribute to the overall characteristics of a breed.

Line-Breeding Successes:

6. Success stories involving line-breeding practices can illustrate how carefully planned matings contribute to the preservation and improvement of breed traits.

**Effective Puppy Placement:
7. Screening Processes:**

Case studies on puppy placements provide valuable insights into effective screening processes. Learn from successful breeders who have implemented thorough application procedures and home visits to ensure the best matches for their puppies.

Long-Term Follow-Ups:

8. Success stories often include long-term follow-ups with puppy buyers. Discover how ongoing communication and support contribute to happy, healthy relationships between breeders and new dog owners.

**Navigating Ethical Dilemmas:
9. Ethical Decision-Making:**

Real-life cases can present ethical dilemmas breeders face. By examining how others have navigated these challenges, you can enhance your own ethical decision-making process in various aspects of breeding.

Transparency in Communication:

10. Successful breeders often emphasize transparency in communication. Case studies highlight instances where open and honest communication with puppy buyers has fostered trust and positive relationships.

Adapting to Industry Changes:
11. Evolution in Breeding Practices:

Case studies provide a historical perspective on how breeding practices have evolved. Understand how successful breeders have adapted to changes in industry standards, technology, and societal expectations.

Navigating Regulatory Landscape:

12. Explore case studies that involve navigating regulatory challenges. Learn how breeders have successfully complied with changing laws and regulations to maintain ethical and responsible breeding practices.

**Applying Lessons to Your Program:
13. Customizing Strategies:**

While case studies offer valuable lessons, it's essential to customize strategies for your unique breeding program. Adapt successful approaches to align with your goals, resources, and ethical principles.

Continuous Improvement:

14. Use case studies as a tool for continuous improvement. Regularly reassess and refine your breeding practices based on the lessons learned from both successful and challenging experiences.

In conclusion, case studies and success stories are powerful tools for breeders seeking to enhance their knowledge and improve their breeding programs. By examining real-life examples, you can gain practical insights into genetics, health management, ethical decision-making, and successful breeding practices. Apply these lessons thoughtfully to contribute to the well-being and success of the German Shepherd breed.

18

RESOURCES FOR GERMAN SHEPHERD BREEDERS

As a German Shepherd breeder, having access to reliable resources is crucial for staying informed, making responsible decisions, and continuously improving your breeding practices. In this chapter, we'll explore practical and easily accessible resources in clear and straightforward language.

Breed-Specific Organizations:

American Kennel Club (AKC):

1. The AKC is a primary resource for breed standards, health guidelines, and information about German Shepherd events. Utilize their website for breed-specific details, educational materials, and participation in conformation events.

The German Shepherd Dog Club of America (GSDCA):

2. The GSDCA is dedicated to preserving the breed's standards and promoting responsible breeding practices. Membership provides access to educational materials, breeder resources, and networking opportunities with experienced breeders.

Health and Genetics:
3. Orthopedic Foundation for Animals (OFA):

OFA offers health testing and certification services. Utilize their database to access health clearances for breeding dogs, especially for hip and elbow dysplasia. This aids in making informed breeding decisions.

Canine Health Information Center (CHIC):

4. CHIC is a centralized canine health database. Participating in CHIC ensures that your breeding dogs undergo comprehensive health screenings. Accessing CHIC records can provide valuable insights into the health history of individual dogs.

Educational Websites and Publications:
5. The German Shepherd Review:

A reputable publication covering various aspects of German Shepherd breeding, including health, genetics, and training. Regularly check for articles and insights from experienced breeders.

The Canine Chronicle:

6. This publication offers a broader perspective on the world of purebred dogs. Stay informed about industry trends, emerging practices,

and noteworthy events within the dog breeding community.

Online Forums and Communities:
7. German Shepherd Forum:

Engage with the German Shepherd community through online forums. Platforms like the German Shepherd Forum provide spaces for breeders to share experiences, ask questions, and learn from each other.

Reddit's German Shepherd Community:

8. Participate in online communities on platforms like Reddit. The German Shepherd subreddit offers a diverse space for discussions, insights, and the exchange of information among breeders.

Webinars and Online Courses:
9. Dog Breeding Webinars:

Explore webinars specifically focused on dog breeding. Platforms like Breeding Business offer webinars covering various topics, from reproductive health to ethical breeding practices.

AKC Breeder Education:

10. The AKC provides online courses for breeders. These courses cover a range of subjects, including genetics, breeding management, and responsible practices. Completing these courses can enhance your knowledge and skills.

Local Veterinary Professionals:
11. Local Veterinary Associations:

Build relationships with local veterinary professionals and associations. Veterinarians can provide guidance on health management, offer insights into breeding challenges, and collaborate on ensuring the well-being of your dogs.

Specialized Veterinarians:

12. Establish connections with specialized veterinarians. Experts in areas such as reproduction, orthopedics, or genetics can offer targeted advice and contribute to the overall health of your breeding program.

**Hands-On Workshops and Events:
13. Canine Reproduction Workshops:**

Attend workshops on canine reproduction. Hands-on experiences provided in such workshops can enhance your practical skills in areas like artificial insemination, whelping assistance, and neonatal care.

Dog Shows and Conformation Events:

14. Participate in dog shows and conformation events. These events offer opportunities to observe expert judges, learn about breed standards, and network with experienced breeders.

In conclusion, accessing resources is fundamental to the success of German Shepherd breeders. Utilize breed-specific organizations, health databases, educational publications, online communities, webinars, local veterinary professionals, and hands-on workshops to continually enhance your knowledge and improve your breeding practices. Staying informed and connected within the breeding community contributes to the well-being of your dogs and the overall advancement of the German Shepherd breed.

GLOSSARY

1. Conformation:

Definition: The overall structure, appearance, and adherence to breed standards in a German Shepherd. Conformation events assess how well a dog conforms to the ideal physical traits specified for the breed.

2. Line-Breeding:

Definition: A breeding practice involving mating dogs with a common ancestor, usually to maintain specific traits or characteristics within a bloodline while minimizing inbreeding.

3. OFA (Orthopedic Foundation for Animals):

Definition: A foundation that conducts health screenings, particularly for orthopedic issues like hip and elbow dysplasia. OFA certifications indicate that a dog has passed these health tests.

4. CHIC (Canine Health Information Center):

Definition: A centralized database that maintains health records of dogs, often used to track health clearances for breeding dogs. Participation in CHIC involves meeting specific health testing requirements.

5. **Whelping:**

Definition: The process of a dog giving birth. Whelping involves multiple stages, including labor, delivery of puppies, and postpartum care.

6. **Genetic Diversity:**

Definition: The variety of genetic traits within a breeding population. Maintaining genetic diversity is essential for the overall health and resilience of the breed.

7. **Stud Dog:**

Definition: A male dog used for breeding purposes. A stud dog should ideally possess desirable traits and conform to breed standards.

8. **Bitch:**

Definition: The female dog, particularly one used for breeding. The term is commonly used in breeding contexts.

9. **Pedigree:**

Definition: A documented record of the ancestry or lineage of a dog. Pedigrees show multiple generations, providing information about a dog's family tree.

10. **Genetic Testing:**

Definition: Analysis of a dog's DNA to identify genetic markers for specific conditions or diseases. Genetic testing helps breeders make informed decisions to reduce the risk of hereditary disorders.

11. **Puppy Socialization:**

Definition: The process of exposing puppies to various experiences, people, and environments to promote positive behavior and adaptability as they grow.

12. **Stud Book:**

Definition: An official record or register maintained by a breed association, listing the pedigrees of purebred dogs. It serves as a reference for breeders and validates a dog's eligibility for breeding.

13. **Heat Cycle:**

Definition: The reproductive cycle in female dogs, also known as estrus. During this cycle, a female is receptive to mating. Understanding the heat cycle is crucial for breeding planning.

14. **Reproductive Vet Specialist:**

Definition: A veterinarian specializing in reproductive health, including fertility, artificial insemination, and pregnancy management. Breeders may consult these specialists for optimal breeding outcomes.

15. **Canine Behaviorist:**

Definition: A professional who studies and specializes in canine behavior. Canine behaviorists provide insights into training, socialization, and understanding the temperament of German Shepherds.

16. **Puppy Buyer Screening:**

Definition: The process of evaluating potential puppy buyers to ensure they can provide a suitable and responsible home for a German Shepherd. Screening involves assessing the buyer's experience, living situation, and commitment to the dog's well-being.

17. **Mentorship Program:**

Definition: A structured arrangement where an experienced breeder guides and shares knowledge with a less experienced breeder. Mentorship programs help transfer expertise and promote responsible breeding practices.

18. **Canine Reproduction Workshop:**

Definition: A hands-on educational event focused on various aspects of canine reproduction, such as artificial insemination, pregnancy care, and whelping assistance.

19. **Genetic Considerations:**

Definition: Evaluating and selecting breeding pairs based on genetic traits, health clearances, and the likelihood of passing on desirable characteristics to future generations.

20. **Responsible Breeding Practices:**

Definition: Ethical and thoughtful approaches to breeding that prioritize the well-being of the dogs, adherence to breed standards, and the betterment of the breed as a whole. Responsible breeding practices encompass health, temperament, and genetic considerations.

This glossary provides key terms and concepts essential for mastering the art and science of breeding German Shepherds. Understanding these terms equips breeders with the knowledge needed to make informed decisions and contribute positively to the breed.

Embark on the rewarding journey of mastering the art and responsibility of German Shepherd breeding. Your dedication to understanding this exceptional breed and implementing responsible practices can positively impact the well-being of these magnificent dogs. Whether you are a novice breeder or seasoned enthusiast, let this guide be your compass. Dive into the chapters, apply the practical insights, and join the community of conscientious breeders striving for excellence. Together, let's elevate the standards and ensure the future health and vitality of the German Shepherd breed. Take the first step—become a beacon of responsible breeding. The legacy you create will resonate for generations to come.